In Defense of the Faith

IN
DEFENSE
OF THE
FAITH

by
W. A. CRISWELL
Ph.D., D.D.

ZONDERVAN PUBLISHING HOUSE
GRAND RAPIDS, MICHIGAN

Grateful acknowledgment is made to the following for permission to use copyright material:

HARPER & ROW, PUBLISHERS
"If Jesus Christ is a Man," by Robert Watson Gilder, taken from *Masterpieces of Religious Verse,* edited by James D. Morrison.

LILLENAS PUBLISHING COMPANY
Lines from "The Love of God," by F. M. Lehman, copyright © 1917 and 1945 by Nazarene Publishing House.

Dedicated
to
THE YOUNG ADULT DIVISION
of the
FIRST BAPTIST CHURCH
in Dallas, Texas,
whose generosity has made
possible the publication
of this volume

FOREWORD

For forty-eight consecutive years the First Baptist Church in Dallas, Texas, has conducted noonday pre-Easter services in a downtown theater. The far-famed pastor, Dr. George W. Truett, preached at these services for twenty-five years. This is now the twenty-third year that I have conducted them. The services are blest beyond any ministry attempted by our congregation. The theater seats twenty-four hundred people and we pack it to its utmost capacity during the week.

This year of 1967 the leadership of the Young Adult Division of our church came to me and asked if they could not publish the series of five messages I delivered during that pre-Easter week. It was a delight to my heart that they would make such a suggestion. I have but the earnest prayer that God will bless them to the reader as fully as He blessed them to the large, listening audience.

Remember, these are delivered, spoken, public messages. They are popular in style, presentation, character. There are a thousand facets in each one that could be dealt with more fully. But a busy lunch hour is hardly a place to be technical or verbose. They represent what we believe about God and our eternal hope in Him. May they bring comfort and encouragement to your heart as we pilgrimage through this world of rejection and unbelief.

Thank you, Johnye Causbie, for typing the manuscript. Thank you Olive Carter, for checking the grammar. And thank you, Young Adult Division, for placing it in the hands of our people. May it be good seed sown in good ground bearing fruit a hundredfold for our Lord.

W. A. CRISWELL

Pastor's Study
First Baptist Church
Dallas, Texas
1967

CONTENTS

In Defense of the Faith

Chapter 1

THE ATHEIST AND THE REALITY OF GOD

Psalm 14:1
The fool hath said in his heart,
There is no God. . . .

Do you think that the Holy Scriptures are full of verses and chapters proving the existence of God? Not so. The atheist is not referred to in the entire Bible except in this one statement in Psalm 14:1 (repeated in Psalm 53:1). Nothing more is said. Nothing else is added. Search the entire Book and that is all. The Bible begins with the tremendous avowal of Genesis 1:1: "In the beginning God created the heaven and the earth." The marvelous message of the Christian faith begins with John 1:1: "In the beginning was the Word, and the Word was with God, and the Word was God." Having stated the overwhelming fact of the existence of the Almighty, the Scriptures thereafter never discuss the possibility of His nonexistence. The reality of God is never argued, never debated, never called in question. The only statement about atheism is this one-half of a verse, "The fool hath said in his heart, There is no God."

Such a fact is astonishing. In our modern world where the existence of God is attacked from every side, we are almost unprepared for the discovery that the Bible does not even discuss the question. There must be some reason for this amazing omission. What could it be? Why do the Scriptures refer to the atheist as a fool, then pass him by with no further notice? Why? Because of, first, his manifest bankruptcy of character. He lives like a fool.

THE ATHEIST'S BANKRUPTCY OF CHARACTER

Perhaps the most famous atheist in America is the woman who was instrumental in persuading the United States Supreme Court to outlaw programs of prayer and Bible reading from the public schools. She described her atheistic triumph in these words:

> I began my attack against Bible reading and prayer in the public schools because of my children. One day

in 1960 my son, Bill, came to me and said: "Mother, you've been professing you are an atheist for a long time. Well, I don't believe in God either, but every day in school I am forced to say prayers." He pointed out to me that if I were a true atheist, I would not permit the public schools of America to force him to read the Bible and to say prayers. He was right. So we began the suit and finally won it when on June 17, 1963, the Supreme Court upheld my contention that prayer and Bible study should be outlawed in the United States public schools.

No doubt about that. As an atheist, she really won her case.

What kind of personal, moral life and philosophy lies back of her atheistic attack? I have before me two newspaper accounts of her addresses before state universities. I have before me an extensive interview published in a national magazine. I shall not insert her blasphemous filth in the body of this address. If you like, you can read some of her sentences published at the end of this chapter, printed for the sole reason that you may see for yourself the moral cesspool created by this philosophy.

But when we carefully examine her position, why should she not live without moral restraints? Morality, righteousness, is grounded in the character of Almighty God. If there is no God, then there is no ultimate, absolute, unchanging right or wrong.

Everything is relative. I may think that stealing is wrong. But the atheist can well say: "That is just *your* idea. I say that stealing is all right." I may say that riot, pillage, civil disobedience and mob violence are wrong. But the atheist can well reply: "That is just *your* idea. I say that such violence is a matter of personal reaction." I may say, "To hurt other people is a great sin." The atheist can most appropriately reply: "That is just *your* idea. I hurt others when I please and as I please." It is only God who makes right eternally right and wrong eternally wrong. Not we. *God.* What we think or say or rationalize does not enter into it. Right is forever right because God made it so. What was right yesterday is right today and will be forever. What was wrong yesterday is wrong today and will be forever. God does not change, and right and wrong are rooted, grounded, founded in an unchanging God. (Compare the words of Jesus in Matthew 19:3-8).

I knew a bank president who one time refused to employ a young man for the bank because he was an atheist. The president was asked to explain his action. He replied that without belief in the judgment of God, all values become relative and he did not want an employee with a relative, changing morality handling the money entrusted to the bank.

"Today," he said, "the young man may be honest. Tomorrow he may change his mind, for honesty without God is a personal whim."

Why do the Scriptures refer to the atheist as a fool, then mention him no more? Not only because of his bankruptcy of character but also because of the empty futility of his speculations. He believes like a fool.

THE EMPTY FUTILITY OF THE ATHEIST'S SPECULATIONS

Ringing through the corridors of the Bible are these clarion words, "The fear [the reverential awe] of the Lord is the beginning of wisdom" (Psalm 111:10; Proverbs 1:7; 9:10). This is forever true. The foundation of every noble life rests upon God. All other superstructures lean upon the wind. The Bible avows that failure to recognize this most primary and fundamental of all facts exhibits the builder as "a foolish man who built his house upon the sand" (Matthew 7:24-27). Not to recognize the presence of God is to be blind in mind and soul as the fool is blind.

A self-important college student said to his eldest brother: "What would you think if I told you that in ten minutes I could produce arguments that would utterly annihilate the Bible?" The brother replied: "About the same thing I would think if a gnat crawled up the side of Mount Everest and said, 'Watch me pulverize this thing with my left hind foot!'"

A hop-toad and a lizard were watching an express train hurtling by in West Texas. Said the hop-toad: "There are fools who believe somebody made that train. Nonsense! It just happened of itself." Said the lizard: "And there are fools who say the thing is run by a locomotive engineer. Such stupidity! It runs by itself." A sand flea overheard the learned discussion between the two, climbed upon one corner of a railroad spike and said: "Some fools say that there is a man called a president who is at the head of this railroad. Such gross credulity! If there is a president of this railroad, I defy him to come and strike me dead!"

God ignores the whole senseless travesty with the one comment, "The fool hath said in his heart, There is no God." Nothing else is added. Nothing else is said. Nothing more in the whole Bible. The atheist believes like a fool.

An atheist never gave an intelligent answer to the vast mystery of the universe. He never gave meaning to a man's life on earth. He denies intelligence, will and personality in creation. He only sees a blind, fortuitous concourse of atoms that created themselves, shaped themselves, and finally produced our minds and souls, without reason, without purpose, without destiny.

But we see order, system, and arrangement everywhere. All we look upon is controlled by invisible forces of gravity, affinity, movement. We have discovered laws of physics, chemistry, astronomy, and a thousand other scientific studies that help lay bare the infinite mind that lies back of the infinitely complex creation. To see the invisible is to discover the secret of all being and reality, whether in matter, mind, or soul.

The answer of the atheist to the questions posited by life and personality found in human beings is sterile and empty. It is like drinking water that does not quench the thirst. It is like eating food that does not satisfy the hunger. It is like building a house without a pattern. It is like reading a book that has no meaning. It is like running a train without an engine. It is like living a life without a purpose. The atheist believes like a fool.

Why do the Scriptures refer to the atheist as a fool, then mention him no more? Not only because of his bankruptcy of character and not only because of the empty futility of his speculations, but also because of his ignoble death. He dies like a fool.

THE DEATH OF THE ATHEIST

One of the great physicists of all times, a professor in a world-famed eastern University, said to the world through the daily newspapers: "I want it clearly understood that I am an atheist. I do not believe in the existence of God. I want no funeral service. I want no service of any kind over my body. I want my remains to be burned and the ashes scattered to the winds." The press carried his words over the world. When he died, his instructions were faithfully followed. His body was burned and the ashes scattered to the wind. Due notice was made thereof by the newspapers of the world, and that was that. Nothing more. Death, the night, the grave, and the long eternal silence became for this man the goal and the meaning of life.

But wait. Could there be something else to be said? I heard a noble, gifted orator from South Carolina describe a visit his mother had made in the years gone by to the cabin of an aged colored "mammy." His mother took along with her the little son, now the marvelous orator. This negro "mammy" had reared his mother and between the two were bonds of deep affection. But the years lay heavy upon the aged colored woman, and she was waiting for the heavenly call. The little boy remembered the dying words of the old "mammy" to his mother.

She said, "Dear Missuz, I iz gettin' ready to trade
this ole, wore-out wagon for a golden chariot."
Think of it! What a glorious way to meet death,
when the trumpets are sounding on the other side
of the river and one of God's saints is crossing over
to home! "Trading this ole, wore-out wagon for
a golden chariot!"

> Swing low, sweet chariot,
>   Comin' for to carry me home!
> Swing low, sweet chariot,
>   Comin' for to carry me home!
>
> A-lookin' over Jordan, what did I see?
>   Comin' for to carry me home;
> A band of angels a comin' after me,
>   Comin' for to carry me home!

We choose between the two: life and death without meaning or purpose; or life and death in the
fullness of the triumph of God. Choose life! As
Moses pled with the children of his people: "I call
heaven and earth to record this day . . . that I have
set before you life and death . . . : therefore choose
life, that both thou and thy seed may live" (Deuter-
onomy 30:19).

> To every man there openeth
> A Way, and Ways, and a Way,
> The High Soul climbs the High Way
> And the Low Soul gropes the Low.

And in between, on the misty flats,
The rest drift to and fro.

. . . .

But every man decideth
The Way his soul shall go.
                    — *John Oxenham*

ADDENDA

These are some of the sentences taken from the published interview with the atheist woman who brought the suit that resulted in the prayer-Bible reading decision of the Supreme Court:

"This would be the best of all possible worlds if everybody were an atheist."

"I am an atheist because religion is a crutch and only the crippled need crutches."

"Religion is irrational reliance upon superstition and supernatural nonsense. Perhaps this sort of claptrap was good for the Stone Age but we are a grown-up world now."

"I will engage in sexual activity with any consenting male any time and any place I damn well please."

The other things she has said are too filthy to publish. I have decided not to repeat the immoral, blasphemous, atheistic remarks she has openly uttered. The fruits of atheism are vile, indeed.

Why would one give himself to such gross darkness? In London there is a society for the promotion of atheism. They used to hold an annual banquet. Upon one of these stated occasions, the president stood up to speak. He began by a reference to the Apostle Paul. He said, "Paul was blinded on the road to Damascus and he remained blind for the rest of his life." The remark brought a burst of laughter and applause from the audience. But the speaker was seen to falter and to fall back into his chair. When they went to assist him, he was dead. The banquet broke up in confusion.

In contrast to the atheist, I think of the godly pastor whom I followed in the pulpit of the First Baptist Church of Muskogee, Oklahoma. He fell asleep in Jesus at his post after a pastorate of twenty-eight years. On his desk was the outline of his sermon yet to be preached. It was entitled "My First Five Minutes in Heaven." What a coronation was his in glory!

Chapter 2

THE LIBERAL AND THE DEITY
OF CHRIST

II *Timothy* 4:3, 4
*For the time will come when they will not en-
dure sound doctrine; but after their own lusts shall
they heap to themselves teachers, having itching
ears;*

*And they shall turn away their ears from the
truth, and shall be turned unto fables.*

The theological liberal has done more to destroy
the faith than all other men who have attacked Christianity through the centuries. The liberal looks upon
the Bible as an antique collection of myths, legends,
and fables. He looks upon Christ as one among
many teachers, philosophers, heroes, and martyrs.
He looks upon God as the great unknowable First
Cause, or as dead.

25

Why is the liberal able to hurt the Christian gospel so deeply? The reason is most plain. If you meet a blaspheming infidel and he says, "God is dead," you are not surprised. If you meet a filthy bum jumping off a freight train in a railroad yard and he says, "God is dead," you are not upset. If you meet a drunken derelict in the gutter on skid row and he mumbles, "God is dead," you are not confused. If you meet a dirty bearded communist revolutionary and he says, "God is dead," you are not troubled. But when a learned professor teaching in a great Christian institution says, "God does not exist," you, being overawed by his scholastic achievements, are therefore doubly confused by his pontifical announcement. You did not expect such an amazing conclusion from a Christian teacher. He is supposed to represent the finest in the faith, and when the faith he represents is depicted as the gospel of an infidel, you are overwhelmed.

THE SLAUGHTER OF THE CHRISTIAN RELIGION

This slaughter of the Christian religion by the liberal theologian is nothing new. It has been going on and growing monstrously through the years. The liberals have destroyed, like a fungus, like a dry rot, the witness of one school after another, one seminary after another, one denomination after another, one mission field after another. Their predatory outreach seemingly has no limits. And all they touch withers away as before a plague.

One of our noble Christian seminaries had a professor who said: "An intelligent man who now affirms his faith in miracles can hardly know what intellectual honesty means. The hypothesis of God has become superfluous in religion. Jesus did not transcend the limits of the purely human."[1] The seminary has been fully captured by infidel teachers exactly like him.

Another great Christian theological school had a professor who said: "We shall hardly bandy words about the finality of Christ. The field is open for anyone at any time to mean more to men than Jesus has meant. He was a mere human being. He was the child of his people and his time." Needless to add, that school also is lost to the faith.

A far-famed Christian college had a professor who wrote: "Whether Jesus ever lived is a historical question that is interesting but it is not fundamental to religion. And if it be suggested in criticism that you then have a Christian religion without a historic Jesus, may I suggest that if Jesus was all that is so generously claimed of him, he ought not to

[1] This and the next seven quotations are taken from Ernest Gordon's *The Leaven of the Sadducees.*

be so sensitive about his own name or himself." This school also has been lost to the faith.

A great seminary had a professor who said: "I believe that the whole view of the Bible with its theory of a chosen people, special revelations, and prophecies is utterly unconvincing and basically vicious." That seminary has been added to the predator's conquests.

Possibly the most famous seminary in America had a professor who said: "I do not believe that the religion of tomorrow will have any more place for prayer than it will have for any other form of magic." And another who said: "As far as I am concerned, the idea of God plays no part in my religion." And another who added, "Where the old religion made the supreme object God, the new religion makes it humanity; sociology takes the place of theology, and an improved social order replaces the belief in immortality." The liberals carried their point and the school and the seminary with them.

The amazing thing is that so few Christian leaders raise their voices in protest to this slaughter. It was not a preacher in a pulpit or a denominational leader who wrote these following words, but an editor of a Chicago daily newspaper in an editorial:

> We are struck with the hypocrisy and treachery of the attacks on Christianity. This is a free country and a

free age and men can say what they choose about religion, but this is not what we arraign these divinity professors for. Is there no place to assail Christianity but a divinity school? Is there no one to write infidel books except professors of Christian theology? Is a theological seminary an appropriate place for a general massacre of Christian doctrines? We are not championing either Christianity or infidelity but only condemning infidels masquerading as men of God and Christian teachers.

This newspaper editorial reminds me of something the famous infidel Bob Ingersol said. He was asked why he had ceased his lecturing against God and the Bible. He replied: "Divinity professors and preachers are doing it better than I. There is no need for me."

An annual report of the American Association for the Advancement of Atheism surely had a right to say: "The liberals are saving the ship of Christianity by throwing her cargo overboard. With what zeal the whole crew of rescuers toss out the Virgin Birth, the Atonement, and the Resurrection! How long will men sail the seas in an empty ship? They will go ashore and enjoy life with the atheists. We welcome the aid of the liberals and pledge them our fullest cooperation in ridding the world of any serious acceptance of Christian theology."

Is not this enough to make the angels weep? I

had a friend who went to the University of Chicago
for a higher degree in pedagogy. While there he
became closely acquainted with a young student in
the Chicago Divinity School. Graduation time came
for them both. The young theologian said to my
teacher friend: "I do not know what to do. I have
been called as pastor of a church in the Midwest.
But it is one of those old-fashioned congregations
who believe the Bible. I do not believe the Bible.
I do not know what to do." My friend said: "I can
tell you what I would do." Our young preacher
eagerly asked, "What?" My friend replied with
deep conviction: "Sir, I would quit the ministry!"
Amen. What place is there in God's kingdom for
a man who does not believe in God? What place
is there in the pulpit for a preacher who does not
believe the Bible? How can a man preach the Gospel if he does not believe in Christ? Yet, these are
the men who have captured so many of our seminaries, who teach in our schools and occupy our
pulpits. No wonder there are historians who refer
to our age as "The Post-Christian Era." God help
us!

A Conglomerate Parade of Present-Day Liberals

In the paragraphs above, we have written of the
liberals who in days past have destroyed most of

the great Christian schools and seminaries of America. Let us now look at the liberals who parade across the magazines and newspapers of this present hour. What a queer, amazing conglomeration they are! And what unbelievable things they say in the name of God! Here before me is a page in a recent issue of a national American magazine [*Time*]. The theology of a famous professor in a Christian seminary is being presented. What does the far-famed teacher believe? I quote:

> For contemporary theologians, God is a dimming concept. "Christian atheists" stand ready to write his obituary. . . . Religion in the past has hindered rather than helped man's self-development. . . . In the future, Christianity may not conceive God as being — which means, literally, that God does not exist since existence is a property of beings only. . . . And, in so far as the word "God" has become a symbol of an outdated supernatural idol, the church may well resign itself to silence as to the name of the being it serves and preaches.[2]

Could an atheist have said it better? Could an infidel have been more pleased?

These last few days we have had abundant opportunity to look closely at these liberals who have captured most of the Christian schools, seminaries, and denominations of America. Just closed has been the

[2] *Time* magazine, December 23, 1966.

eight-day annual session of the Christian Education Division of the National Council of Churches. It was attended by about one thousand church education leaders from forty denominations. Great notables from the ends of the theological world were present to address the assembly. What a spectacle for men and angels to behold! (Or, over which to weep!)

One far-famed bishop stood up to say with pontifical solemnity that Sunday schools are "dangerous." He added, "There is grave doubt that any Sunday school anywhere is of any benefit." Then he went on to make it clear that he was opposed to Sunday schools that teach the Bible.

The associate executive secretary of the Texas Council of Churches reported that to his horror they had discovered that devotionals are being held in seventy percent of Texas public schools. Then he threatened, "We may have to delete devotionals in public schools, district by district, in court action." The next morning an editorial in the *Dallas Morning News*[3] commented: "It is odd, to say the least, that the Texas Council should be so concerned over praying in the classrooms. . . . There are problems a plenty in our man-made world that cry for the attention of

[3] February 16, 1967.

Christians. We can't believe that devotionals in schools are one of them."

But the real headliner of the National Council of Churches is yet to be presented. When he appeared, his picture and his message filled the front page of the daily newspapers. "Why do I wear a clerical collar?" he said. "Because I don't have to wonder what I'm going to wear in the evenings. I don't have to pick out neckties." He continues: "As to the church, it's idolatrous. You can't worship there. As to the sacraments, you can baptize with spittle. People don't understand the sacraments. I look at the eyes of fathers and uncles who say, 'Let's get the hell out of here; there's a TV show I want to see.' "

His remark about baptizing with spittle intrigued me. Jesus walked all the way from Nazareth in Galilee to the Jordan River, where John was baptizing, in order to be baptized by the Baptist preacher in the flowing waters. If one can baptize in spittle, that's a lot of spit! It reminded me of the sign in a warehouse which read: "Don't smoke. Remember the Chicago fire." Underneath, some wag wrote: "Don't spit. Remember the Johnstown flood!"

But this cleric is not yet done. He solemnly says, "I can't yet bring myself to say Jesus [is] Christ." Then he cannot be saved. The Scriptures plainly say in Romans 10:9: ". . . if thou shalt confess with thy mouth the Lord Jesus, and shalt believe in thine heart that God hath raised him from the dead, thou shalt be saved." I Corinthians 12:3 avows: ". . . no man can say that Jesus is the Lord, but by the Holy Ghost." Any man, even if he wears a clerical collar, who refuses to accept Jesus as Lord and Christ is outside the door of salvation. He has never been regenerated. There is no salvation apart from the acceptance of Jesus as the Son of God, the Saviour of the world (Acts 8:36-39).

FIVE FACTS AFFIRMING THE DEITY OF CHRIST

In spite of all that liberal "Christian atheists" have to say in denial of the deity of Christ, there are five great facts that affirm His Godhead. The first is the fact of His birth. The "protevangelium" in Genesis 3:15 says that the seed of the woman shall bruise (crush) Satan's head. But a woman does not have "seed." Only the man has "seed." The old Rabbis, through the centuries, pondered that Messianic promise and wondered what it could mean. But the prophets made it clear. Isaiah wrote in 7:14: ". . . Behold, a virgin shall conceive, and bear a son, and shall call his name Immanuel [God is with us]." The same prophet added in a further revelation: "For unto us a child is born, unto us a son is given: and the government shall be upon his shoulder: and his name shall be called Wonderful, Counsellor, The mighty God, The everlasting Father, The Prince of Peace" (Isaiah 9:6).

Seven hundred fifty years after Isaiah delivered this prophecy, the angel Gabriel was sent to a city in Galilee called Nazareth, to a virgin Jewess named Mary to announce to her that she should be the mother of this foretold, foreordained child. "The Holy Ghost shall come upon thee, and the power of the Highest shall overshadow thee: therefore also that holy thing which shall be born of thee shall be called the Son of God" (Luke 1:35).

An unbeliever could come to me and say: "Sir, if an unwed mother were to avow to you that her child was born of the Spirit without an earthly father, would you believe it?" My reply would be: "Yes — if the birth of that child was foretold thousands of years before. Yes—if when the child was born the angels sang, and the star of promise stood over the place where the infant lay. Yes—if when the child were grown he had power over the wind and the waves, over disease and death. Yes — if when he was slain, the third day he was raised from the dead. Yes—if when he ascended to heaven his disciples, through the centuries, were numbered by the millions and the increasing millions." Yes, a child like that could surely, truly be virgin-born according to the Word of God.

The second great fact affirming the deity of Christ is His life. He presented the credentials of deity. By fiat God spoke the worlds into existence: the sun, the moon, the starry skies. By the same fiat, Jesus the Christ controlled the worlds above Him, around Him, and before Him. He merely spoke the word and the dead were raised to life, the blind could see, the lost were saved, and human flesh saw the glory of God.

The third great fact affirming the deity of Christ is His death. He ". . . died for our sins according to the scriptures" (I Corinthians 15:3). If Christ Jesus were a man like us, He would have had to die for His own sins. Because He was perfect, blameless, sinless, without spot or blemish, as the Lamb of God chosen before the foundation of the world, He could die for us, bearing our sins in His own body on the tree (I Peter 1:20; 2:24). Only God could bear our sins away. To forgive sin is not the prerogative of man. It pertains to deity alone, and the sin-forgiving Jesus has the prerogatives of deity.

The fourth great fact affirming the deity of Christ is His resurrection. According to Romans 1:4 He was "declared to be the Son of God . . . by the resurrection from the dead." According to Hebrews 1:3,

". . . when he had by himself purged our sins, [he] sat down on the right hand of the Majesty on high." Thus the author of Hebrews could triumphantly add in 7:25: "Wherefore he is able also to save them to the uttermost that come unto God by him, seeing he ever liveth to make intercession for them." Thus Paul could write in Romans 5:10: "For if, when we were enemies, we were reconciled to God by the death of his Son, much more, being reconciled, we shall be saved by his life."

Affirm it for yourself whether Christ be living or not. Try praying to Jupiter, Jove, Juno, Janus, or to any other of the gods of old. Attempting such a thing would make us feel foolish. Try calling on the name of Alexander the Great, Augustus Caesar, Washington, or Lincoln. Such an act of appeal would be ludicrous in the extreme, a travesty in the name of religion. But try calling upon the name of Jesus; try praying in the name of Jesus. There is answer; there is power; there is the presence of God. "For whosoever shall call upon the name of the Lord shall be saved" (Romans 10:13).

The fifth great fact affirming the deity of Christ is His return. Jude 14 announces: "Behold, the Lord cometh with ten thousands of his saints." The text of the Revelation is stated in 1:7: "Behold, he cometh with clouds; and every eye shall see him, and they also which pierced him: and all kindreds of the earth shall wail because of him. Even so, Amen." Revelation 11:15 triumphantly adds: "The kingdoms of this world are become the kingdoms of our Lord, and of his Christ; and he shall reign for ever and ever." We feel like saying with the poet Richard Gilder:

> If Jesus Christ is a man,
>   And only a man, I say,
> That of all mankind I will cleave to him,
>   And to him will I cleave alway.

> But if Jesus Christ is a God,
>   And the only God, I swear
> I will follow Him through heaven and hell,
>   The earth, the sea, and the air.

Or as the Psalmist so beautifully writes it (24:9, 10):

> Lift up your heads, O ye gates;
> Even lift them up, ye everlasting doors;
> And the King of glory shall come in.

> Who is this King of glory?
> The Lord of hosts, he is the King of glory.

And that Lord is our Lord forever and ever, even the God-man Christ Jesus.

Chapter 3

THE COMMUNIST AND THE
LIVING CHURCH

II Timothy 2:19
Nevertheless the foundation of God standeth
sure, having this seal, The Lord knoweth them
that are his. . . .

With this subject, "The Communist and the Living Church," I feel as one attending a massive, world-wide funeral service. I feel as one standing with bowed head before the burial of a civilization, a nation, a people, awaiting the great resurrection day of the Lord. As one of the brokenhearted mourners, I cry the lament of Jeremiah: "Is it nothing to you, all ye that pass by? behold, and see if there be any sorrow like unto my sorrow, which is done unto me, wherewith the Lord hath afflicted me in the day of his fierce anger" (Lamentations 1:12). The slaughter and the decimation of the Christian churches by ruthless communist predators is unparalleled in the annals of the human race.

For the first time in the history of mankind the communists have brought into being a monstrous type of government; namely, nations that are openly, avowedly, statedly atheistic. No ancient Greek would make a destiny-determining decision without first consulting the oracle at Delphi. No ancient Roman would go to war without first propitiating the gods. But these bow at no altar; they call upon the name of no deity. Their cry is, "Religion is the opiate of the people"; and again, "God does not exist, why worship him?"

The Churches in Russia and Other Communist Lands

The communist implementation of this bitter atheism is tragic beyond compare. Who has ever looked upon such sorrow? In our recent visit to Russia, we arrived in Leningrad in the middle of a Saturday night. Early the next morning, the Lord's Day, I arose and went for a walk in the center of the city where our hotel was located. At the corner of the first street intersection was a church building. It had been turned into a railway station. I continued down the street. Within a few blocks I saw another church edifice. It had been turned into a granary. Down the avenue I walked to the next church. It was a warehouse. Others I saw were boarded and locked and falling into ruins. It hurt my heart to look upon such desecration.

Two world-famed cathedrals are located in Leningrad. One is the Kazan cathedral, spacious, beautiful, with winged rotundas that open in front like welcoming arms. But inside, alas, it has been turned into a "cathedral of atheism." It houses a public display that ridicules the idea of God. Where the high altar once stood is a statue of Lenin. Engraved on the wall behind are the cardinal precepts of communism. Every part of the vast building is filled with "demonstrations," "proofs," of the nonexistence of God. A bronze piece of statuary exhibits the scornful attitude of the party toward the church. A heavy, heavy cross is crushing beneath its interminable weight a poor mother and child. Instead of the cross being a symbol of victory over sin and death, it is here in the Kazan cathedral portrayed as an instrument of oppression. Only a diabolical mind could have so conceived it.

The other great, world-famed cathedral in Leningrad is St. Isaacs, the largest in Eastern Europe and the house of worship for the Czars. The Sunday I was there a woman scientist was demonstrating, with a long pendulum swinging from the middle of the vast and lofted dome, the rotation of the earth. Exhibits of the conquest of communism were on display in every part of the beautiful edifice, but none rivaled the blasphemy of the area where once stood the high altar. On one side was a picture of the Russian cosmonaut Titov. On the other side was the picture of the Russian cosmonaut Gagarin. On the wall above were written these words in Russian, in German, in French, and in English: "We have searched the heavens and there is no god."

The heavy hand of atheistic communism is never lifted from the people from the cradle to the grave. In the streets of every city can be seen bands of little kindergarten children, each child holding on to the clothing of the youngster in front of him as they cross the intersections. From birth they are taught to be atheists. The children up to eight years of age are Octoberists and are privileged to wear a red star. From eight to fourteen years of age they are "Young Pioneers" and wear a red handkerchief. Beyond fourteen years of age and through twenty-eight years of age they are Komsomols or "Young Communists." It is no wonder that the child never knows the name of God and the worship of the Almighty. He is taught that such faith is empty superstition.

In each of the great cities of Russia a church is open. Since all the other churches have been closed by government decree, why is one left intact? I asked a faithful band of worshipers in one of these city churches that question. A Latvian uprooted from his home and sent to work in a Russian factory instantly replied: "I'll tell you why. If the government closed all the churches it would openly advertise to the world the emptiness of their boast of religious freedom. Therefore in each city one church is left open so that when a visitor comes from abroad and asks to attend a church, the communist agents take him to the congregation and say, 'See, here in Russia we have full freedom of worship!' "

What freedom! One church in a city the size of Chicago! One church in a city the size of New York! The property is owned by the state. The church operates under the surveillance of the state. The financial program of the congregation is under the direction of the state. There can be no Sunday schools, no Bibles, no publishers of literature. There can be no seminaries for the training of preachers. There can be no educational program of any kind. There can be no evangelistic meetings, no invitation, no propagation of the Gospel whatsoever. It is a chained, oppressed, outcast congregation.

No answer to atheism is permitted. A blasphemous infidel book was placed in my hands in Odessa. I looked through it. It was cheap, hollow, empty. I said to the communist agent: "We could answer every argument in this sterile volume easily and with convincing facts." He replied: "But in our glorious country only the truth can be propagated. This book is the truth. Here in Russia falsehood cannot be propagated and religion is falsehood." It is that simple to the atheistic communist. And that tragic!

In other communist lands, as in Asia, we can only guess at the wanton destruction of the churches of our Lord. In North Korea during the two years of 1959 and 1960 more than three million of her citizens were liquidated, including all known Christians. As far as we know, there is no openly surviving church in North Korea. What has happened to the Christians in China, only God could know. Word has come that the Red Guards in uncontrolled fanaticism have persecuted unto death the remaining Christians. The tragic story is written in blood.

The Imponderable in the Judgment of Almighty God

Where is God in this merciless onslaught? He still lives. He still reigns. The story is not done yet. The final chapter is yet to be written. The imponderable in this world sweep of atheism is the Almighty Himself. Let us read again Luke 20:17, 18: "And he beheld them, and said, What is this then that is written, The stone which the builders rejected, the same is become the head of the corner? Whosoever shall fall upon that stone shall be broken; but on whomsoever it shall fall, it will grind him to powder." A harbinger of this coming judgment can be terribly seen in the destruction of the Baptist Church in Riga.[1]

In the heart of Latvia's capital city stood a Baptist Church with its tall, tall steeple, a lofty spire topped by a cross of wood covered with gilded metal. In 1940 the Soviet Union, in violation of its treaty with the little country, sent her Red Armies crashing into the Republic. Many thousands, including the most prominent religious leaders, were herded into boxcars like cattle and deported to Siberian labor camps. The Nazi Armies came; then again the Red Army, and Latvia became a slave state of the Soviet Union.

In the summer of 1961 a Russian "inspector," an agent of the secret police, sat in the office of a local communist official in Riga. Pointing toward the

[1] This incident taken from O. K. Armstrong, *Religion Can Conquer Communism,* pp. 24-26.

lofty steeple topped with the cross on the Baptist
Church, he rasped: "How does it happen, comrade,
that you permit that symbol of superstition to stand
in this city?" The Latvian of the Soviet regime explained that the Baptist congregation contained some
influential citizens and to close the church would
bring unfavorable reactions from the public. "You
set a bad example, comrade, for the youth of the
city," said the commissar. "They must be taught that
religion is superstition and reaction. Besides, your
city needs another cultural center and that audito-
rium would make a good TV and drama house."
The first Sunday in September, 1961, the Baptist
congregation gathered for the last time in that be-
loved church home and tearfully sang:

> Blest be the tie that binds
>   Our hearts in Christian love;
> The fellowship of Christian minds
>   Is like to that above.
>
> We share our mutual woes,
>   Our mutual burdens bear;
> And often for each other flows
>   The sympathizing tear.
>
> When we asunder part,
>   It gives us inward pain;
> But we shall still be joined in heart,
>   And hope to meet again.
>   — *John Fawcett*

The Soviet commissar left with this final address: "Tear off that steeple so the building will never look like a church, but first *cut down that cross.*"

One morning a squad of workmen under a communist boss appeared with ladders and tools to cut down that gilded cross. None of the workmen would volunteer to destroy it. The foreman cursed and scolded, but none moved toward the unhappy assignment. Finally a young man, a leader of the Komsomol (Young Communist League) stepped from the crowd. He would cut down the cross. It proved to be a difficult job. When his legs became numb, he climbed back down to the roof to rest himself. Back up again he went and hacked away the back of the cross sufficiently for the ropes held to it from below to pull it to the ground. Crashing to the earth, the cross fell. In the next instant, the Komsomol's safety belt broke loose and he came falling spread-eagle from the steeple to the hard pavement below. With a sickening thud he fell by the cross, dying in a widening pool of blood. The foreman, ashen and shaken, dismissed the men. Within an hour a car carted away the remains of the would-be hero, now a cadaver for some medical school. The next day a squad of Russian Army engineers came with a huge battering ball and demol-

ished the steeple. Today the edifice, shorn of its state-
ly spire and cross, is a TV station and dance hall.

Under such heartbreaking persecution, does the
church live? Does God still have His own? Yes,
a thousand times yes. Some of the churches, as in
the communist countries of Russia and Eastern Europe, can be seen if diligent search is made. They are
assigned by the government to out-of-the-way places
almost always behind high, ugly walls. The people
for the most part are poor, old, despised, pitiful.
Never have I cried in my life during a church service
as I did in the Baptist Church at Leningrad. The
plaintive hymns, the people kneeling in prayer with
hands outstretched to heaven, and the weeping of the
congregation moved my soul to its depths. In one
part of the service the pastor read letter after letter
which brought a flood of tears from the people. I
asked the Intourist Agent why the people were cry-
ing so. The agent replied that these letters were
from families who had renounced the faith, had left
the church, but who had repented and were asking
the church to forgive them and to receive them back
into the fellowship of the fold. They were coming
back home. The tears were tears of joy and welcome.

Some of these open churches are hurt by the
government in their very souls. In one of the famed

Baptist Churches in the capital city of a communist country behind the iron curtain, we found the people deeply divided over their present pastor. Their former pastor had been sent to a small village on the frontier, there in practical exile to starve to death or to live as he could. His family still remained in the home congregation. The newly assigned pastor is looked upon as a collaborator. Sadness, sorrow, frustration, I found everywhere.

THE UNDERGROUND CHURCH WITH HER MARTYRS

Beyond these open churches I found evidences again and again of an underground church. There are people and pastors who refuse to comply with the heavy rules of their atheistic government and rather than conform, they meet in forests, in caves, in hidden places. Out of Siberia one such group, about thirty-five in number, came to the American Embassy seeking asylum. The world did not know they existed until then. The whole earth was moved with pity by their plight. But the American ambassador explained to us that he and our government were helpless. There was nothing they could do for those ragged, oppressed, pitiful people. The Kremlin assured the American ambassador that they would be returned to their homes without persecution or penalty. They were taken away by the Red police and no amount of effort on the part of our ambassador can discover what became of them.

Oh, the price in blood, suffering, and martyrdom those Christians pay for their love to Jesus. I think of the church at Smyrna, the martyr church, the only church of the seven addressed in Asia with whom the Saviour found no fault.

> And unto the angel of the church in Smyrna write: These things saith the first and the last, which was dead, and is alive; I know thy works, and tribulation, and poverty, (but thou art rich) and I know the blasphemy of them which say they are Jews, and are not, but are the synagogue of Satan. Fear none of those things which thou shalt suffer: behold, the devil shall cast some of you into prison, that ye may be tried; and ye shall have tribulation ten days: be thou faithful unto death, and I will give thee a crown of life. He that hath an ear, let him hear what the Spirit saith unto the churches; He that overcometh shall not be hurt of the second death (Revelation 2:8-11).

Our fellow Christians in these communist lands are loyal unto death. The Roman coliseum stands as a symbol of the suffering martyrdom of the first century Christians. The Red flag with its hammer and sickle is a symbol today of the red, red blood poured out in devotion to Christ by those who name

His name beyond the iron and the bamboo curtains. And the end is not in sight. A rough band of Chinese soldiers, atheistic and God-hating, gathered a little congregation of Christians inside their church building and brought them out one by one. If the Christian renounced his faith in Jesus, he was liberated. One by one they refused to renounce their Saviour and one by one they were all beheaded. The last to be brought to the door was a small boy. The leader of the soldiers said to the lad: "You are so small. Why don't you live? I am placing a picture of Jesus on the ground. You grind it into the dust with your heel and we shall let you go." The little boy looked at the picture of the Saviour on the ground, then up to the Lord in heaven and said: "Lord Jesus, one time you died for me. This time I shall die for You." With these words he placed his head before the sword of the murderous executioner, and the last member of the little church was slain.

> The Son of God goes forth to war
>   A kingly crown to gain.
> His blood red banner streams afar,
>   Who follows in His train?
>
> A noble army, men and boys,
>   The matron and the maid,
> Around the Saviour's throne rejoice
>   In robes of light arrayed.

They climbed the steep ascent of heaven
Through peril, toil, and pain.
O God, to us may grace be given
To follow in their train.

— Reginald Heber

Chapter 4

THE MATERIALIST AND THE
END OF THE WORLD

Hebrews 11:1, 3

*Now faith is the substance of things hoped for,
the evidence of things not seen.*

*Through faith we understand that the worlds
were framed by the word of God, so that things
which are seen were not made of things which
do appear.*

American culture is becoming increasingly secular. Our goals of achievement, both for the individual and for society as a whole, are largely materialistic. Our goals are those of technology and scientific research which in turn can produce for us an endless stream of gadgets. We interpret life by the world's standard of success, and we proceed as if God did not exist. We live for status symbols and the indulgence of fleshly appetites. We worship the trappings of the affluent society. Our sense of values is lost in the miasmic quagmire of empty possessions.

The proverbial rich Texas tycoon wrote in his will that when he died he wished that his body be buried in his goldplated Cadillac. When that inevitable time came, the huge crane lifted up the shining automobile containing the remains of the deceased millionaire and swung around to deposit them both in the gaping hole of a grave. In the awe and hush of that dramatic moment an onlooker was heard to whisper, "Man, ain't that livin'!" When his widow, a far-famed Dallas dowager, later arrived at the pearly gates the gatekeeper asked to see her credentials for entrance. She proudly laid before him a Neiman-Marcus charga-plate, an annual membership card in the Brook Hollow Country Club, a ticket to the Dallas Symphony Orchestra, and a citation from the Cotton Bowl Association for her loyal support. The gatekeeper dutifully took full cognizance of all the tokens of cutural and civic achievement and then said: "Well, come in. But I'm tellin' you now, you ain't gonna like it here!"

Americans are essentially materialistic. Evil stalks our nation as well as the world. The dramatic symptoms of our decaying civilization can be seen in the increasing secularization of education, the rising crime rate, and the amoral background of every level of our society. The harbinger of our ultimate dissolution can be seen in our wild orgies on beach and campus, in the punks, beatniks, dope addicts, alcoholics and irresponsible vandals who roam our streets, and in the sick readers of sick books and the sick viewers of sick movies. The soul of America has been sullied and dispirited by plenty, fouled and misbegotten by pleasure, and caught in the sterile junk-web of so-called science.

LEARNING FROM HISTORY

We never seem to learn from the past. The wrecks of nations washed up on the shores of human history apparently are unable to teach us anything in our time and age. How empty, how temporary, how transitory are material achievements! Let us read again the proud boast of King Nebuchadnezzar recorded in Daniel 4:30: "Is not this great Babylon, that I have built for the house of the kingdom by the might of my power, and for the honour of my majesty?" Have you seen it? It is a mound of dust, a pile of mud, a conglomerate of rubble.

The famous sonnet of the English poet Percy Bysshe Shelley entitled "Ozymandias" bears the same tragic message.

I met a traveler from an antique land
Who said: Two vast and trunkless legs of stone
 Stand in the desert. Near them, on the sand,
Half sunk, a shattered visage lies, whose frown,
 And wrinkled lip, and sneer of cold command,
Tell that its sculptor well those passions read
 Which yet survive, stamped on these lifeless things,
The hand that mocked them, and the heart that fed:
 And on the pedestal these words appear:
"My name is Ozymandias, king of kings:
 Look on my works, ye Mighty, and despair!"
Nothing beside remains. Round the decay
 Of that colossal wreck, boundless and bare
The lone and level sands stretch far away.

Of both Nebuchadnezzar and Ozymandias and
of all other materialists, the poet Thomas Gray did
write:

The boast of heraldry, the pomp of power,
And all that beauty, all that wealth e'er gave,
 Await alike th' inevitable hour.
The paths of glory lead but to the grave.

The sorrow of sorrows in the world-view of materialism is that it leaves out God. What greater
tragedy is there than that we should lose God and
not miss Him? The reality of God has nearly dis-
appeared from the average daily American life. On
an airliner a man was working a crossword puzzle.
Suddenly he looked bewildered. He inquired, "What
is a word of three letters with 'o' in the middle mean-

ing man's best friend?" His friends looked amused. They chorused in unison, "dog." That's the likely answer you would get, too. The man worked on at the puzzle. "I think the last letter must be 'd,'" he sounded out. But nobody got it. Maybe they did not want to be the first with the revolutionary thought that it could be "God."

THE MATERIALIST AND THE WORLD AROUND US

In materialistic philosophy there is no place for God. The materialist believes that matter, physical substance, is all there is in the universe and that all phenomena, including mind and personality, are due to physical agencies. The materialist believes that in the beginning something came out of nothing and that that something shaped itself, evolved itself, designed itself into the present universe as we look upon it today. He believes that the end will come in the same unintelligible way. As the universe began in a gathering of atoms without meaning, so shall it end in a scattering of atoms without purpose. When the force of the sun burns out, that will bring eternal night and everlasting death. To him there is no other answer and no other meaning.

Let us examine this world-view of materialism more closely. Let us look at his explanation of the beginning of the universe and then let us take a moment to evaluate his prognostication of the ending of creation. First, we scrutinize his presentation of the beginning of the solar system.

A materialist says to me: "That is a fine watch you have there. Where did it come from?" I reply: "I plucked the parts out of nowhere, placed them in a box, shook them for two hours, opened the lid, and there in all its beauty lay this excellent watch." When the man looks at me as though I were an idiot, I hasten to add: "Perhaps I shook the box for more than two hours. Would you believe six?" "Surely," he says, "you are jesting. Such a procedure is unthinkable." "But," I reply, "you believe that the solar system and life itself came into being in just such a way." "Oh, but that is different," he observes. Is it? Are you sure it is different?

The universe, in its laws and planets and orbits, is so precise that the Elgin Watch Company boasts that "We set our time by the stars." The whole solar system is far more intricate and exact than the finest jeweled watch ever assembled. Who did it? "It was an accident," says the materialist. The orbit of the earth around the sun is in a precision according to the weight and size of the sun and the motion and distance of the planet earth from the burning orb. If any of the multitudinous factors were changed, the whole would collapse. "But this is an accident." Well and good. Let us assume these multitudinous imponderables were all accidents. The same laws of distance, weight, size, and motion govern the orbit of the moon around our earth. "But this is another accident." Well and good. The same laws of weight and motion and distance govern the other eight planets around the sun and the scores of moons that circle those planets. Are they all accidents working together? It begins to look as if somebody made the watch. It begins to look like a master plan. But a master plan would involve a Planner and the materialist cannot admit that.

One of the basic concepts in physical phenomena is that of "entropy." Entropy refers to the degree of disorder in a system. One of the principles of thermodynamics states that the entropy of a system tends to increase. For example, if a poem is set up in type and the type is disturbed, the shaking will result in a more disorganized arrangements, not in a more sublime poem. It is thus with our solar system. If the system is disturbed, the result will not be a better arrangement but a more disorderly one. But the materialist replies, "Anything can happen if time is not a factor and time is limitless." Excellent. Since time is no factor, try shaking in a box the type set up for Tennyson's "Crossing the Bar." The law of entropy takes over. Entropy increases.

Disarrangement increases. But time is no factor. Try shaking the box for a hundred years. Try shaking the box for a thousand years. Try shaking the box for a hundred thousand years. Without the guiding hand of intelligence, the box will never produce the beautiful poem by the Victorian Poet Laureate of England. But the materialist says, "The poem 'Crossing the Bar' is too complicated." Well and good. Try shaking in a box the type set up for "Mary Had a Little Lamb." The more the box is shaken, the more disorganized the poem becomes.

Intelligent Planning in Creation

Verses of poets are extremely simple compared with the complexities of the universe. Watches manufactured by men are child's toys compared with the minute arrangements of the planetary systems. Any deviation from intelligent planning would result in the abysmal disorganization of the whole. We have an example of that in the first chapter of Genesis. Genesis 1:1 states, "In the beginning God created the heaven and the earth." Whatever God created must have been beautiful, perfect, complete, well done. But something tragic happened for Genesis 1:2 states, "And the earth was [became] without form, and void; and darkness was upon the face of the deep. . . ." Isaiah 45:18 and Jeremiah 4:23

declare to us that God in the beginning did not create our earth waste and uninhabitable. Something must have happened. What could it have been? The entropy of sin entered God's universe. Lucifer fell and with him the plague of sin destroyed God's glorious creation. There was disorganization, entropy of systems, everywhere. Could a million, billion years of accidents remake God's world? No. Read the last part of Genesis 1:2, "And the Spirit of God moved upon the face of the waters." Intelligence, planning, purpose brought order out of chaos.

This intelligent planning of God we see everywhere and in all things. Psalm 139:14 says that we are "fearfully and wonderfully made." The anatomy, the metabolism, and the very processes of existence of the human body are a full commentary upon God's skill in creating the physical frame of a man. Look at one tiny part of our intricate life; namely, the clotting of blood, without which no man could live. The process of the clotting of the blood begins when the blood is exposed to air and the blood platelets deteriorate, forming a substance which acts as a trigger to start the reaction. Thromboplastin is formed and reacts with prothrombin, helped on by accelerator globulin (ac-globulin) and calcium ions, to form thrombin. Prothrombin was previously synthesized by the liver. The thrombin reacts with fibrinogen, a soluble protein in the blood also produced by the liver, to form fibrin, an insoluble protein, which starts the clotting. How did the liver know it was supposed to produce both prothrombin and fibrinogen to prepare for an emergency it had never experienced? How did the platelets in the first place happen to contain the right substance to start the reaction? Is all this, and a million other miracles like it, blind accident? Or is it the work of intelligence? The materialist has no answer. He dares not answer.

THE CHRISTIAN LIGHT OF HOPE

We need but the moment that remains to us to delineate the philosophy of despair that characterizes the materialist as he looks toward the future and the end of the world. Nothing awaits us, according to him, but death, darkness impenetrable, frustration, and defeat. To him life has no meaning and the grave is the final goal toward which all men inexorably are turning. There is no light, no hope, no immortality, no resurrection, no heaven, no God, no Saviour, no triumph beyond death. He lives in a world of abject defeat whose dark night is unbroken by even a small gleam of hope. We cannot sow the wind and not reap the whirlwind.

We cannot thrust God out of our lives and out of our universe and find peace for our souls. Surely, surely, there must be some other way than that of the materialist. Surely there must be some other explanation, some other revelation. Could there be? There is.

The story of the conversion of the Angles of Northumbria by Paulinus forms one of the most vivid passages in the history of the Venerable Bede, early English historian. The scene is laid in his own native country. The time is just a few years before Bede was born, in the early 7th century A.D. Paulinus, the missionary sent to Northumbria from Canterbury, has presented the claims of the Gospel to King Edwin and his warriors. After the plea of Paulinus, King Edwin sits in silence at the head of the council table, in the great hall. Then one of his aged warrior-sages arises and says: "Around us lies the black land of night." Someone has put his words from Bede's record into poetry.

> Athwart the room a sparrow
>   Darts from the open door.
> Within the happy hearth-light
>   One flash and then no more.
> We see it come from darkness
>   And into darkness go —
> So is our life, King Edwin;
>   Alas, that it is so.

But if this pale Paulinus
    Have somewhat more to tell;
Some news of whence and whither,
    And where the soul will dwell,
If on that outer darkness
    The sun of hope may shine,
He makes life worth the living:
    I take his God for mine.

And thus our English forefathers became Christians. And thus God has blest us with light for our darkness, resurrection for our death, victory for our defeat, heaven for our home.

Chapter 5

THE SINNER AND THE SACRIFICE ON THE CROSS

I Corinthians 15:1-3

Moreover, brethren, I declare unto you the gospel which I preached unto you, which also ye have received, and wherein ye stand;

By which also ye are saved, if ye keep in memory what I preached unto you, unless ye have believed in vain.

For I delivered unto you first of all that which I also received, how that Christ died for our sins according to the scriptures.

There are two kinds of Christianity. There is a Christianity of social improvement, of economic amelioration, of civic betterment. If Christ is preached at all, He is presented as a great humanitarian, a noble reformer, a magnificent martyr. If its disciples use the word "salvation," they mean

65

a reconstruction of the social order. Confucius was a great teacher, contributing to the welfare of society. Socrates was a great teacher, contributing to the welfare of society. Aurelius and Justinian were great teachers, contributing to the welfare of society. And Jesus was a great teacher, contributing to the welfare of society. He was nothing more, except possibly the best among many peers.

There is, also, another kind of Christianity. It is a Christianity of redemption. In this message God in heaven was moved by the tragic plight of a lost human race, a race condemned to die by judgment upon their sins. In mercy and in love God came down in human flesh and took upon Himself our sins and died in our stead. Through faith in this atoning Christ we are forgiven our iniquities, we are restored to God's favor, we are saved from eternal penalty of our transgressions. Simon Peter spoke of that marvelous salvation like this: "Christ also suffered for us, . . . who his own self bare our sins in his own body on the tree, . . . by whose stripes ye were healed" (I Peter 2:21-24) And again he wrote: ". . . ye were not redeemed with corruptible things, as silver and gold . . . but with the precious blood of Christ, as of a lamb without blemish and without spot: who verily was foreordained before the foundation of the world" (I Peter 1:18-20).

In the Christianity of social improvement, the death of Christ is but an incident, though a moving devotion. In the Christianity of redemption, the death of Christ is the cardinal truth around which all other truths revolve. Take away the death of Christ from the first type of preaching and the preacher is not particularly troubled. In fact, he would like to rid the volumes of theology and the hymn books of any reference to such blood and suffering. To him the preaching of the cross is an offense, a part of a religion of the shambles and of the butcher shop. Take away the death of Christ from the second message and there is nothing left. The preacher no longer possesses the "good news," the evangel of the forgiveness of our sins. There no longer remains any hope of heaven nor any promise of the world to come.

Which of these two kinds of Christianity is the Christianity of the New Testament? Undoubtedly, it is the Christianity of the cross. "But God forbid that I should glory, save in the cross of our Lord Jesus Christ . . ." (Galatians 6:14).

At the heart of the Christian faith is the cross; the cross in all its naked hideousness, as the Roman would have it; the cross in all its philosophical irrationality, as the Greek would have it; the cross in all its shame and offense, as Paul describes it. "I

declare unto you the gospel . . . by which also ye
are saved . . . how that Christ died for our sins according to the scriptures" (I Corinthians 15:1-3).
"And, I, brethren, when I came to you, came not
with excellency of speech or of wisdom, declaring
unto you the testimony of God. For I determined
not to know any thing among you, save Jesus Christ,
and him crucified" (I Corinthians 2:1-2). If it is
the Christianity of the Book, it is the Christianity
of the cross.

> At the cross, at the cross, where I first saw the light,
>   And the burden of my heart rolled away.
> It was there by faith I received my sight,
>   And now I am happy all the day.

The First and Great Doctrine of the New Testament

Look closely at that passage from Paul in I Corinthians 15:3: "For I delivered unto you first of
all that which I also received, how that Christ died
for our sins according to the scriptures." What does
he mean by the words "first of all"? His reference
has not so much to do with time as with importance.
As there is a first and great commandment of the
law, so there is a first and great doctrine of the New
Testament. What is that tremendous and primary
teaching? It is not the fatherhood of God. It is not

the kingdom of heaven. It is not the Incarnation. It is the atonement of Christ for our sins. The doctrine of the vicarious expiation of our sins by the death of Christ is the very keystone of grace, the very heart of the Gospel. No other truth stands so high. In the center of the ancient Roman Forum stood the golden milestone. From it the vast network of Roman roads poured out to the ends of the civilized world. To it all the roads in the Empire eventually led. Every milepost was numbered by distance from that central Forum. As "all roads lead to Rome," so all the great doctrines of the Holy Scriptures lead to the cross.

A critic one time said to Charles Haddon Spurgeon, "All your sermons sound alike," to which the world-famed London preacher replied, "Yes, I take my text anywhere in the Bible and make a beeline to the cross." There is no pardon without atonement; there is no remission without the shedding of blood; there is no reconciliation without the payment of debt. Not by the beauty of holiness of His life, but by His stripes we are healed. Such events as the birth of Jesus, His temptation, His transfiguration, His institution of the Lord's Supper, even His ascension into heaven are omitted from one or more of the four gospels. But they all, in fullest detail, relate His suffering and death. He came into the world, He was born in a human body conceived by the Holy Spirit, in order that He might offer in His own flesh a sacrifice for our sins.

> For it is not possible that the blood of bulls and of goats should take away sins. Wherefore when he cometh in the world, he saith, Sacrifice and offering thou wouldest not, but a body hast thou prepared me: In burnt offerings and sacrifices for sin thou hast had no pleasure. Then said I, Lo, I come (in the volume of the book it is written of me,) to do thy will, O God. . . . By the which will we are sanctified through the offering of the body of Jesus Christ once for all (Hebrews 10:4-7, 9, 10).

The preaching of the atoning death of Christ is the distinctive, determining doctrine of the New Testament. It differentiates our faith from all other religions. The Christian message is distinctively one of redemption. Its fundamental purpose is to recover man from the bondage and judgment of sin. The Christian religion is not in the first place an ethic, although it is ethical. It is not in the first place a theology, although it has a theology. It is not in the first place reformational, although it has social, cultural, and political overtones. It is first and above all a Gospel of redemption, an announcement of the good news that God has for Christ's sake forgiven us.

My sins, oh, the bliss of this glorious thought,
 My sins, not in part but the whole,
Are nailed to the cross and I bear them no more,
 Praise the Lord, praise the Lord, O my soul!
         — *H. G. Spafford*

The symbol of the Christian church is not a burning bush, however that might declare the living presence of Jehovah. It is not a table of stone on which are engraved the enduring commandments of God. It is not a seven-branched lampstand casting rays of light throughout the world. It is not a halo around a submissive head. It is not even a crown of splendid triumph. It is a cross—a rugged, naked, heavy cross. Here is the spectacle for men and angels to behold. Here the sinner looks for salvation, the Christian for confidence and strength.

> And you, being dead in your sins and the uncircumcision of your flesh, hath he quickened together with him, having forgiven you all trespasses; blotting out the handwriting of ordinances that was against us, which was contrary to us, and took it out of the way, nailing it to his cross; and having spoiled principalities and powers, he made a shew of them openly, triumphing over them in it (Colossians 2:13-15).

Have you been to Jesus for the cleansing power;
 Are you washed in the blood of the Lamb?
Are you fully trusting in His grace this hour;
 Are you washed in the blood of the Lamb?

> There is life for a look at the crucified One.
> There is life at this moment for thee.
> Then look, sinner, look unto Him and be saved,
> Unto Him who was nailed to the tree.

THE SCRIPTURES AND THE ATONEMENT OF CHRIST

Particularly notice that Paul says, "Christ died for our sins *according to the scriptures." According to the Scriptures.* All the thousands of years of history recounted in the Bible are "His-story." They speak of Him; they tell of Him; they prepare for Him who was "the Lamb slain from the foundation of the world" (Revelation 13:8). The burden of the Old Testament message is the atonement of Christ. It is the scarlet thread through every book. The blood of the innocent animal slain in the garden of Eden spoke of Him (Genesis 3:21). The sacrifice of Abel, whose blood was mingled with his offering, spoke of Him (Genesis 4:8). The offering of Isaac by his father, Abraham, was a picture of Him (Genesis 22:1-14). The sprinkled blood of the Passover Lamb was a type of Him (Exodus 12:1-14). The Levitical offerings portrayed Him. "For the life of the flesh is in the blood: and I have given it to you upon the altar to make an atonement for your souls: for it is the blood that maketh an atonement for the soul" (Leviticus 17:11). The daily sacrifice in the Tabernacle and in the Temple was a harbinger of Him (Hebrews 10:1-14). The message of the prophets depicted Him.

> But he was wounded for our transgressions, he was bruised for our iniquities: the chastisement of our peace was upon him; and with his stripes we are healed. All we like sheep have gone astray; we have turned every one to his own way; and the Lord hath laid on him the iniquity of us all. Yet it pleased the Lord to bruise him; he hath put him to grief: when thou shalt make his soul an offering for sin, he shall see his seed, he shall prolong his days, and the pleasure of the Lord shall prosper in his hand. He shall see of the travail of his soul, and shall be satisfied: by his knowledge shall my righteous servant justify many; for he shall bear their iniquities (Isaiah 53:5, 6, 10, 11).

The burden of the New Testament message is the atonement of Christ. The keynote of the whole gospel story is sounded by John the Baptist in his introduction of Christ: "Behold the Lamb of God, which taketh away the sin of the world" (John 1: 29). The four gospels proclaim this message of redemption in their very form. They are not biographies of Jesus. They are made up of selected words and incidents arranged according to the purpose of the author (John 20:30, 31; 21:25). Yet over one-fourth of the space in the gospels is given to the last few days, yes, hours, of His life. There are a thousand interesting events of His career passed over. There are a thousand marvelous discourses delivered by Him which are never mentioned. Why? These all were omitted in order to leave abundant room for the story of His death.

As soon as Jesus began His public ministry, He began to speak of His coming death. In John 2:19 He said, "Destroy this temple, and in three days I will raise it up." The Jews did not understand what He meant, but we do. In John 3:14, 15 He said: "And as Moses lifted up the serpent in the wilderness, even so must the Son of man be lifted up: that whosoever believeth in him should not perish, but have eternal life." Nicodemus did not understand what He meant, but we do.

In John 6:51-57 Jesus said:

> I am the living bread which came down from heaven: if any man eat of this bread, he shall live for ever: and the bread that I will give is my flesh, which I will give for the life of the world. The Jews therefore strove among themselves, saying, How can this man give us his flesh to eat? Then Jesus said unto them, Verily, verily, I say unto you, Except ye eat the flesh of the Son of man, and drink his blood, ye have no life in you. Whoso eateth my flesh, and drinketh my blood, hath eternal life; and I will raise him up at the last day. For my flesh is meat indeed, and my blood is drink in-

deed. He that eateth my flesh, and drinketh my blood, dwelleth in me, and I in him. As the living Father hath sent me, and I live by the Father; so he that eateth me, even he shall live by me.

Those who heard Jesus say this were utterly baffled by what He meant. But we understand.

In John 12:20-33 the Greeks who had come to Jerusalem requested of one of the disciples, "Sir, we would see Jesus." The Lord replied, "And I, if I be lifted up from the earth, will draw all men unto me." The people, not understanding, asked, "How sayest thou, The Son of man must be lifted up?" They could not comprehend it. But we do. As John 12:33 reads, "This he said, signifying what death he should die."

In John 12:1-8 is recorded the story of Mary's anointing of Jesus at the supper in Bethany. Jesus said, "Against the day of my burying hath she kept this." The disciples did not understand it. But we do. He came into the world to die for our sins. The cross was ever before Him.

The tremendous, everlasting emphasis of our Lord upon His death can be clearly seen in the institution of the Lord's Supper.

And as they were eating, Jesus took bread, and blessed it, and brake it, and gave it to the disciples, and said,

> Take, eat; this is my body. And he took the cup, and gave thanks, and gave it to them, saying, Drink ye all of it (Matthew 26:26, 27).

Christ worked many miracles, yet never did He say, "This miracle is wrought for the remission of sins." Christ healed many sick, yet never did He say, "This healing is bestowed for the remission of sins." Christ preached many sermons, yet never did He say, "This sermon is preached for the remission of sins." Christ was tried and tempted, yet never did He say, "This trial is borne for the remission of sins." But He did say, "This is my blood of the new testament, which is shed for the remission of sins" (Matthew 26:28).

What is the one event in the life of our Lord that He asks, above all, that we remember? It is His death.

> For I have received of the Lord that which also I delivered unto you, That the Lord Jesus the same night in which he was betrayed took bread: And when he had given thanks, he brake it, and said, Take, eat: this is my body, which is broken for you: this do in remembrance of me. After the same manner also he took the cup, when he had supped, saying, This cup is the new testament in my blood: this do ye, as oft as ye drink it, in remembrance of me. For as often as ye eat this bread, and drink this cup, ye do shew the Lord's death till he come (I Corinthians 11:23-26).

The burden of the message of the apostles was the atoning death of Christ for our sins and His glorious resurrection for our justification. He was delivered for our offenses and raised for our justification. In the shadow of the cross they took their stand to preach the Gospel of the Son of God. In the New Testament they left behind, every leaf and every word is inspired by His suffering and stained by His blood. It was the message of Peter (I Peter 1:18-20). It was the message of Paul (I Corinthians 2:1, 2; Galatians 2:20). It was the message of John.

> But if we walk in the light, as he is in the light, we have fellowship one with another, and the blood of Jesus Christ his Son cleanseth us from all sin. . . . And he is the propitiation for our sins: and not for ours only, but also for the sins of the whole world (I John 1:7; 2:2).

This will be the burden of our ascription of praise to the Lamb throughout all the ages of eternity. "Unto him that loved us, and washed us from our sins in his own blood, and hath made us kings and priests unto God and his Father; to him be glory and dominion for ever and ever. Amen" (Revelation 1:5b, 6).

> And they sung a new song, saying, Thou art worthy to take the book, and to open the seals thereof: for thou

wast slain, and hast redeemed us to God by thy blood out of every kindred, and tongue, and people, and nation; and hast made us unto our God kings and priests: and we shall reign on the earth. And I beheld, and I heard the voice of many angels round about the throne and the beasts and the elders: and the number of them was ten thousand times ten thousand, and thousands of thousands; saying with a loud voice, Worthy is the Lamb that was slain to receive power, and riches, and wisdom, and strength, and honour, and glory, and blessing. And every creature which is in heaven, and on the earth, and under the earth, and such as are in the sea, and all that are in them, heard I saying, Blessing, and honour, and glory, and power, be unto him that sitteth upon the throne, and unto the Lamb for ever and ever. And the four beasts said, Amen. And the four and twenty elders fell down and worshipped him that liveth for ever and ever (Revelation 5:9-14).

THE GOOD NEWS OF OUR HOPE AND SALVATION TODAY

The cross of Christ, the atoning grace of our Saviour, is the good news of hope and salvation that we preach today. What do you see when you look at the cross? The priests and the elders who delivered Him to Pontius Pilate saw an enemy destroyed. They rubbed their hands in eminent self-satisfaction. They had aboundingly accomplished their goal.

What do you see when you look at the cross?

The quaternion of Roman soldiers saw five garments to be divided, one to each of the four, and the fifth to be gambled for at the place of His execution.

What do you see when you look at the cross?

The curious by-standers heard His cry for "Eli" (God), but not fully understanding His language, they thought He called for the prophet Elijah. They, therefore, sat down and watched to see if Elijah would come, probably betting for and against it.

What do you see when you look at the cross?

One of the malefactors crucified with Him turned his head to look upon another criminal dying like himself, and in blasphemous language he reviled and abused Him.

What do you see when you look at the cross?

The other malefactor looked upon the Saviour and saw a precious forgiveness that promised hope for another world. He asked Jesus, "Lord, remember me when thou comest into thy kingdom" (Luke 23:42).

What do you see when you look upon the cross?

John saw atonement and cleansing in the blood and the water that poured from the wounded heart.

What do you see when you look at the cross?

God saw His only begotten Son, dying for the sins of the world.

What do you see when you look at the cross?

We see a revelation of the sin in our hearts that nailed Him to the tree. Who pressed upon His brow that crown of thorns? We did. Who drove those nails through His hands and feet? We did. Who thrust that iron spear into His side? We did. We all had a part. We slew the Prince of Glory.

A dreamer one time looked in a vision upon the scourging of Christ. The executioner brought down upon the back of the Saviour the thick, heavy lash studded with jagged pieces of lead. As he struck with all his strength, blood flowed down from the open wounds. As the dreamer watched, he could stand the suffering no longer. He rushed forward to seize the raised arm of the soldier and as he did so, the executioner turned and looked in surprise at the dreamer. The dreamer recognized — himself! O God, what our sins have done to Jesus!

What do you see when you look at the cross?

We see a revelation of the love and sacrifice of Jesus for us. Were I the only lost sinner in the world, He still would have come down from heaven to suffer in my stead, to die for me.

> O love of God, how rich and pure,
>   How measureless and strong!
> It shall forever more endure,
>   The saints' and angels' song.
>
> — *F. H. Lehman*

Tigranese, King of Armenia, was taken captive by a conquering Roman army. The defeated king, along with his wife and all his children, was brought before the Roman general for the sentence of death. Tigranese threw himself on his knees before the conqueror and pleaded for the lives of his family. He said to the victorious Roman: "Take me and do anything you like with me, but spare my wife and children." His appeal so moved the general that he set the entire family free. As they journeyed away from the Roman headquarters, Tigranese turned to his wife sitting by his side, and said, "What did you think of the Roman general?" She replied, "I never saw him." Tigranese exclaimed, "You never saw him! You were standing in his presence. Where were your eyes?" She said, "They were fixed upon the one who was willing to die for me. I saw no one else."

> Were you there when they crucified my Lord?
> Were you there?
> Were you there when they crucified my Lord?
> Were you there?
> Oh, sometimes it makes me to tremble, tremble, tremble,
> Were you there when they crucified my Lord?

What do you see when you look at the cross?

We see our victory over sin, death, hell, and the grave. Through the veil of His flesh, torn asunder,

we have our entrance into heaven. Sin no longer
has dominion over us. The grave can no longer
hold us. Hell no longer is a fear for us. We are
more than conquerors through Him who loved us
and gave Himself for us.

"O death, where is thy sting? O grave, where is
thy victory? The sting of death is sin; and the
strength of sin is the law. But thanks be to God,
which giveth us the victory through our Lord Jesus
Christ" (I Corinthians 15:55-57).

What do you see when you look at the cross?
God's call to our hearts.

> *Hoc feci pro te*
> *Quid facis pro me.*
> This have I done for thee.
> What hast thou done for me?

Surely, Lord, my life, my soul, my all belong to
Thee.

> Was it for crimes that I have done
>   He groaned upon the tree?
> Amazing pity, grace unknown,
>   And love beyond degree!
>
> But drops of grief can ne'er repay
>   The debt of love I owe.
> Here, Lord, I give myself away,
>   'Tis all that I can do.
>
> — *Isaac Watts*

SUBJECT INDEX

83

SCRIPTURE INDEX